• MEET •

ROSA BONHEUR

Read With You
Center for Excellence in STEAM Education

Read With You

Published by Read With You Publishing. Printed in the United States of America.

ISBN: 979-8-88618-292-7
First Edition December 2022

I'm Rosa Bonheur, a French painter who loves to paint animals! I painted fur carefully here. What animal do you think it is?

Trace the little hairs that go every direction. Do you think its fur is soft or stiff?

Wild Cat, 1850

I loved painting and learned from my father, who was also a painter.

My pictures impressed people. I was only 19 when my art was first shown in a gallery!

A Limier Briquet Hound, c. 1856

Women were not allowed to go to art school when I was born. But my father believed in my talent.

He built the only free drawing school for girls in Paris. My sister and I taught many girls to combine nature and their imaginations to make amazing paintings.

Highland Raid, 1860

What animal is this? How does this animal make you feel?

Check the title to find out! That is the name for a boy deer.

A Stag, 1893

There is a special word in my language for someone who draws animals. It's *animalière*.

I also sculpted animals when I was younger. But my brother, Isidore, was much better at it than I was!

The Horse Fair, 1852-1855

I worked hard at painting realistic, believable animals. Can you see the light on the fur here?

If you paint the light and shadows just so, it feels like you can reach in and touch each animal's skin!

Two Horses, 1842

Do you remember seeing this animal before? How are the colors in his fur different here?

Fur reflects light differently at sunset! Any color looks like a rainbow when the sky is full of pink and yellow.

The Call of the Stag, c. 1890-1899

Animals are so fun to paint! Get a brush and paint your favorite ones.

Changing Pastures, 1863

Find Examples

Bonheur made sculptures as well as paintings. This sculpture is *Lion*, c. 1880.

Compare this sculpture with Bonheur's animal paintings. How are they different?

How do both the sculpture and the paintings make the animals look like they are moving?

Compare the lion's mane with the fur of the other animals in this book. How does Bonheur draw different fur textures?

Is there an animal that isn't in this book that you would like to see Rosa Bonheur paint?

Rosa B

Connect

This painting is *The Wounded Eagle*, c. 1870.

Have you ever been this close to a bird?

What do you think is the hardest part of the bird to draw?

What is your favorite part of this painting?

If you could draw a furry mammal or a flying bird, which would you choose? Why?

Rosa Bonheur

Craft

Option 1

1. Write the letters of your name on blank flashcards.

2. For each letter, draw an animal that starts with that letter on the other side of the card.

3. For a bigger challenge, try the whole alphabet!

Option 2

1. Find paper and pencils and choose a photo of your favorite animal.

2. Practice drawing the animal's fur, feathers, skin, or scales. Sketch its body parts.

3. When you like your sketches, draw your animal on a new piece of paper using what you learned in practice.

Explore fun facts about interesting painters by visiting
https://www.readwithyou.com/pages/meet-the-artist-activities